Beginners Gu
Raising Chi

Complete Up To Date, No Fluff Guide On How To Raise A Happy Backyard Flock

Yolanda Barrett

Introduction

Do you have an interest in raising chicken?

Have you tried raising chicken before but, it did not work out for you?

Or

Are you raising your chicken, but you are finding the process hard and complicated?

If you've answered YES, then look no further.....

In this book, I will guide you and take you on a step by step journey on how to:

- Raise your chicken

- **Handle your chicken**

- Choose the right breed

- **Build the appropriate shelter for your chicken**

- Feed your chicken on a daily basis

- **Treat your chicken when they get sick**

- Prevent sickness from catching your chicken

- **Protect your birds from predators**

And all the other knowledge that you require to raise a healthy, happy, and productive flock of chicken.

So get comfortable as possible, get your reading spirit on board and brace yourself to take this journey with me, and I promise you, it will be like an experience you have never had before.

Before delving into this matter, firstly, allow me to enlighten you on a few words that I have used in this book that you might find new. Many of these are common regular words you have heard before, but you have probably found them confusing at times.

The words include:

- Hen: a female adult chicken

- Rooster: a male adult chicken

- Chick: a baby chicken of either sex

- Pullet: a female chick (immature chicken)

- Cockerel: a male chick (immature chicken)

- Broody: a hen inclined or wishing to incubate eggs

- Non-Setting: a hen that does not have the inclination or wish to incubate eggs

- Dual purpose: chicken practical for meat and egg production

- Coop: a chicken shelter

You can refer to these words if you are confused to stop the confusion.

Let's begin.

Table of Contents

The first thing you need to do before you start raising chicken is to understand the type of chicken you will rear based on your interest on whether you want eggs, meat, beauty, or a blend of these benefits.

So I will begin by highlighting some of the common breeds of chicken, including what each one offers, growth rate, what it is best known for, and other important information will make it easy to choose your chicken.

A Comprehensive Introduction To Chicken Breeds

So what is a chicken breed?

A chicken breed is a group of chicken that have similar or identical characteristics or features.

They are grouped into different types of breeds based upon:

- Their body type or shape

- The color of their feathers

- The number of their toes

- Amount of feathering

- Based on whether they have feathered shanks or not.

There are hundreds of chicken breeds all around the world. In this book, I will discuss the most common and available chicken breeds that you can easily find.

They include:

- ISA Brown or the golden comet. It is a hybrid

- Plymouth Rock

- Barnevelder

- Australorp

- Naked neck

- Orpington

- Silkie

- New Hampshire red

- Frizzle

- Belgian d'Uccle

- Rhode Island Red

- Polish

- Cochin

- Leghorn

- Sussex

- Araucana

- Wyandotte

Let us group these breeds based on what they are best known for.

1. Best Breeds For Egg Production

The best breeds for mass egg production include:

1. Lohmann Brown

This is a brown or silver-white breed of chicken with a single comb.

This breed will start laying eggs at 18 weeks, and they will give you 300 eggs per year for ten years. They lay medium to large eggs (larger than all the other breeds), and their eggs are brown.

2. Hybrid

Breeds such as the golden comet, also known as ISA brown, is a golden brown chicken and has soft white tail feathers. The female feathers are brown or bronzy buff in color with stripes, while the male ones are light yellow.

This breed of chicken matures fast, and they start to lay eggs at a younger age than most chicken (around 16 weeks of age). They lay around 250-320 eggs per year.

Their eggs are medium-sized and are brown colored.

So if you are looking for the best layer, this one here is one of the best there is.

3. Rhode Island Red breed

This breed of chicken originated from Massachusetts. Their feathers range from deep red to black, some having a mixture of brown and black feathers. Mature chicken weighs around 3 to 4 kg.

They begin laying eggs at about 18 to 20 weeks of age, and they will give you up to 260 eggs per year.

Their eggs are also brown and are medium-sized.

4. Leghorn Breed

Leghorn breed has a full white body and a large thick red rose comb or single comb. This breed will start giving you eggs at 18 to 21 weeks of their age. They reach their peak egg production when they are eight months old and will lay approximately 250 eggs per year (sometimes a little more). Their eggs are white and medium-sized eggs, but their eggs grow bigger as the hen ages.

This breed will serve you for 4 to 6 years.

5. **Sussex Breed.**

This breed has around eight different colors, but the most common ones have a pure white body with black neck and tail feathers. The average mature female weight is 3.2 kilograms and male 4.1 kilograms. They begin to lay eggs at 20 weeks of age and will give you around 250 eggs per year. These eggs are large enough and vary from brown to creamy white color. This breed will serve you for about eight good years.

6. **Plymouth Rock**

This breed has grey feathers with white stripes all around their body. They start to lay eggs when they are about sixteen to twenty weeks old. They will give you around 200 eggs per year.

They produce eggs after every 25 hours. Their eggs are medium-sized and are light brown.

This beautiful bird will serve you for 6 to 8 years.

7. **Barnevelder**

This is a predominantly black chicken with brown tipped feathers. Mature hens weigh 5 to 6 lbs. while mature roosters weigh 7 to 8 lbs.

They will start laying eggs when they are 18 to 20 weeks old. And they will give you around 200 eggs per year for 4 to 7 years.

These eggs are small to medium-sized and are light brown.

<u>Egg production in your chicken will depend upon the following factors</u>

- The breed that you will choose to raise. As seen above, the different breeds produce eggs differently. Some lay more eggs per day, whereas others provide a seemingly less amount of eggs.

- Egg production will also depend upon how you will manage your pullets before they start laying eggs. To obtain a good amount of eggs, you will need to feed them well, water them well, provide them with a comfortable nesting area and a good shelter.

- Light management is also an essential factor in egg production. Adequate lighting (about 16 hours per day) will be reciprocated with more eggs.

- Feed your chicken well if you want more eggs. A feed that has all the nutrients required by the chicken is what you should give them.

- Last but not least, the amount of spacing in the shelter that your birds live in also determines how many eggs they yield. Make your chicken comfortable, and they will reciprocate that with more eggs.

2. Best Breeds For Meat

1. Cornish Cross

Cornish cross chicken is a hybrid of Cornish chicken and white Plymouth chicken. It is a moderately heavy, large and muscular bird. The feathers are closely knit together, giving it a more slender appearance that might fool your eyes.

They come in a variety of colors. They can be white, buff, or a mixture of brown and blue.

These breeds are fast growers, faster than all the other breeds of chicken. And in just 6 to 8 weeks, they would have grown to a point where they weigh approximately 12 lbs.

They tend to eat a lot but for a good course, because all that they eat is turned into muscle.

They have broad breasts, larger thighs, and legs set far apart, and also they have enriched yellow skin.

2. **Jersey Giant**

Jersey giant is a broiler (chicken raised for meat) that originated in the state of New Jersey in the 1800s. It is available all around the world now, and you can get it anywhere.

This breed comes feathered in black. Sometimes the black feathers take on a green sheen within their black color. Some come in white color too but not so many.

This chicken is large, practically the largest breed. It is a no brainer why they are called "Giant." They grow very slowly and eat quite a lot. It takes them approximately 8 to 9 months to reach maturity but two years to fully grow. Therefore, you won't have any other choice but to be patient with this breed.

The hens weigh 9 to 11 lbs. with a height of 16 to 20 inches, while cocks weigh 11 to 15 lbs. with a height of 22 to 26 inches. And their meat is dark and rich in nutrients.

They live for about six years.

3. Bresse

The Bresse is a French breed (they originated from France). They made their first appearance in the USA in 2011, but you can find them now in the US, as people have been moving them around globally.

They come feathered in all white with blue colored feet and a single red comb. They can also come in black, grey, splash and blue.

This breed has been praised for their delicious meat and to spice things up more; their bones are quite thin and dainty, which means much of its weight is pure meat.

They are known to grow fast and mature in 16-20 weeks. The cocks weigh 2.5 to 3 kg, while the hens weigh 2 to 2.5 kg.

4. **Orpington**

Orpington chicken originated in Britain in 1866.

They have a light brownish yellow fluffy feathers. But you can find some that are black, blue or white. Their comb is red and they do have five pointed tips.

They have are heavy birds, with a short and broad body. They mature in 18-24 weeks and weigh approximately 8 to 10 lbs.

They are known for their amazing flavor and tenderness in their meat.

5. <u>Freedom Ranger</u>

Freedom ranger, just as their name suggests, are free-ranging breeds that search widely for their food in a nearby pasture or just around your compound.

They are red with several black-spotted feathers. They grow so fast, and in just about 9-11 weeks, they are mature and weigh approximately 5 to 6 pounds.

Their meat is tender and succulent with more of yellow Omega 3 fat and less saturated fat than the other fast-growing breeds of chicken.

With their free-ranging spirit, you will find them easy to raise because they can flourish on low protein feeds and thrive on food scouting than the Cornish crosses; they also have stronger immunity and will rarely fall sick.

6. **Buckeye Chicken Breed**

It originated in the USA, Ohio estate in the late 19th century. Their primary color is mahogany red, and they have a pea-like comb.

They become mature and ready to serve you with their delicious meat in just 16 to 21 weeks and weigh 9 pounds.

They are known to be disease resistant and can easily survive any weather.

With good nutrition and proper care, you are guaranteed that your chicken will give you healthy and delicious meat there is, but if you want to spice things up and get better, there is a new technique that you can use.

This technique is known as:

3. Caponization

Caponization is the castration of male chickens.

This castration is the removal of the testes. It is advisable to castrate your roosters only if you are raising them purely for meat production.

If you are up for this, you should do it when a chick is still small, that is, when the chick is aged between 6 weeks to 3 months. This is because while immature, the gonads are small and are much easier to remove. If you wait until your roster has reached sexual maturity, the gonads would have developed, become large, and too close to the kidneys. This will hinder the safe removal of these testes.

So how do you do this?

- First of all, before you caponize your chicken, you will have to withhold food and water for about 24 hours. By doing this, you will keep the intestines empty, allowing you to see the testicles clearly.

- Restrain your chicken in the safest possible way.

- Locate the last two posterior ribs, spread them gently and carefully to see the testicles then make an incision between them.

- Remove the furthest testicle first: then remove the closest one after. This is important because in case of a bleed, the blood won't obstruct your vision of the second testicle.

- Finally, free your chick, feed them well, and allow them to heal.

When the testes are removed, the cockerel fails to develop specific male characteristics, or they tend to lose those characteristics if they have developed already.

Caponized often have a slow growth rate but the upside of that is that they accumulate more body fat and have juicier and tender light and dark meat.

The meat of a regular rooster that has not been castrated tends to become stringy, a little coarse and even tough as the rooster ages. You won't notice a decline in the quality of meat with capons.

So if you want the best meat ever of your chicken, you will have to pick a few of your young male chicks, castrate them, and wait for the tastiest chicken meat ever.

4. The Best Breeds For Both Production Of Meat And Eggs

Most of these breeds have been discussed earlier, so I will simply just state them.

They include the following;

1. Leghorn chicken – they mature in 16 to 21 weeks and weigh 5 to 6 pounds. And they produce 280 eggs per year.

2. Turken (Naked Neck Chicken) – they mature in 11 to 18 weeks, weighing 4 to 6 pounds. They also produce 104 eggs per year.

3. Buckeye breed – they are normally raised for meat production because of how delicious they are but they also produce 200 eggs per year.

4. Chantecler – They mature in about 11 to 16 weeks, weighing 7 to 9 pounds. They also produce 200 eggs per year.

5. Plymouth rocks

6. Orpingtons

7. Wyandottes.

8. Black Australorp – They mature after 18 months and lay 250 eggs per year. They also produce good meat and weigh from 2.5 kg to 4.5 kg.

5. Best Breeds For Show And Plumage

1. Silkie

Silkie is a very beautiful breed of chicken known for its fluffy white plumage. Their plumage feels like silk and satin, and it lacks barbicels. This makes their feathers to feel so smooth. They are smaller in size as compared to other breeds. They are friendly, calm, and very docile. They are the best companion you could ever ask for.

This bread has a few unique qualities, such as:

- They have five stores instead of four like most breeds

- They have black skin and bone

- They have blue earlobes

- They also have black meat.

Silkie chickens need tender, loving care. They need more attention to keep them looking smart and sassy. They can get messy when wet because their fluffy feathers do not dry easily.

2. **Black Shumen**

29

Black Shumen is a very rare breed of chicken from Bulgaria.

It has the following unique features:

- Totally black feathers

- Greenish sheen

- A single comb

- White skin and

- Red earlobes

- Low body weight as compared to other breeds of chicken

3. **<u>Polbar Chicken</u>**

This breed of chicken is of Polish origin. It was created by crossing the American Plymouth Rock and the native polish Green-legged Partridge.

This chicken has a very beautiful plumage as shown in the picture above.

4. <u>Wyandotte</u>

The feathers of the Wyandotte breed of chicken are simply state of the art. They are popularly described as show birds. It comes in a variety of colors, but the common ones have a brown, blue or salmon ribbon in color with an outlining or a frame of black.

Their comb is also red in color and rosy in shape.

5. Barnevelder

This breed is also another beauty. They have beautiful feathers that are double lace of brown and black. Each feather has rings of alternating brown and black color with a final black ending.

Their stylish feathers make them unique and a perfect breed for plumage.

6. Ameraucana

This is an American breed chicken.

These chicken have unique features such as:

- They lay blue eggs

- It is bearded, tailed and muffed

- They do not have wattles, and if they do, it is very small

- They have feathered feet

- They have ear tufts. Ear tufts are simply feathers, which generally grow from the slender, fleshy flap, right below the ear.

They come in various colors giving you a chance to choose which color you like most.

7. **Frizzle**

This is a unique breed of chicken with feathers curling upward and outward from their bodies. This unique appearance of their feathers occurs because the shaft of their feathers twists and curls from when they are a very little chick.

This breed is fun, conspicuous, and lovable and are beautiful to watch.

Frizzle chicken requires special care because the frazzles are extremely delicate. Their feathers can be so brittle, in that, they can break at touch.

8. Cochin

Cochin chicken is another breed of unique chicken. They have big bodies, weighing up to 5kgs. They are very beautiful chicken to look at and are heavily feathered all the way down to their feet. They come in a vast array of colors such as white, black, blue, partridge, and buff.

Cochin is the gentlest breed of chicken and has a very friendly chicken. You will love them; I promise you that.

They do not move far from their coop, giving you an easy time to watch them.

Now that you have a good understanding of the chicken breed options, let's move to the next step, which is buying/selecting the chicken.

Buying Of Chicken: How To Do It Like The Pros

Now that you have carefully decided on which breed you will want to raise based on your preferences, go to your nearest best chicken shop, a hatchery, or any local farmer nearby and buy the breed that you want. Be careful to know the basic features of the breed you want because most of these breeds look the identical, and you might end up raising something different.

You can buy chicken in any of these 3 states:

- A fertilized egg and that you incubate in a chicken incubator until it hatches.

- A chick (most people buy a day old chick)

- Or a fully grown chicken

Buy a combination of both male and female chicken so that they can reproduce.

Before you buy the chick or the adult chicken that you will need, you must inspect the chicken to see if they are healthy.

You can do this by checking the following:

- Check if they are sleepy or lethargic, i.e., if they have reduced activity or alertness

- If they are reluctant to move

- If they have any nasal or eye discharge

- If they are coiled and hunched into a ball like manner

- If they are reluctant to eat

If the chicken you are interested in exhibits any of these signs, you should refrain from buying it.

Now that you have got the chicken of your choice, where will they shelter?

In the next chapter, I have discussed everything you need to know about your chicken shelter.

Building A Chicken Coop

In this chapter, we will learn how to build a chicken coop (the shelter for your chicken).

But before we do that, there are a few factors that you have to put into account first before we start building.

1. Factors/Requirements For Your Coop

- Sufficient space for your chickens

- Proper ventilation

- Protection from external predators, harsh weather conditions

- The right temperature, comfortable enough for your chickens

- Quality roosting perches for your chickens

- Adequate lighting.

- Nesting boxes for laying eggs

- Appropriate floor material

- Feeders and drinkers

- And finally, do you have a good spot for the place that you will build your coop. The perfect spot should have proper drainage systems, shade, etc.

We will discuss each of these factors and what you need to do for your chicken to grow perfectly.

2. Coop Space

You should ensure that you have a space large enough for your birds. I would recommend that you have at least 2-3 ft. square for every chicken inside the coop and 8-18 ft. square for every chicken in an outside run. A chicken run is simply the fenced or enclosed area outside the coop that your chicken can walk, play or roam around at.

Adequate space is important because it prevents fighting or pecking at each other, bullying, cannibalism, or sometimes even death.

Very close confinements encourage stress and are a potential for disease among your chicken.

Another important factor is that you should allow room for expansion in your coop in case your flock grows.

It is important to note that your coop size or space requirement can vary depending on factors such as:

- The age of your flock. Little chicks do not require as much space as the adult ones.

- The climate or the season: In the cold season, chicken usually like to be close together for heat purposes.

- The breed of your chicken. Some breeds can handle small spaces or confinement (breeds such as Plymouth Rocks, Australorps, Orpingtons) while other breeds require adequate spaces.

- How often are they able to get out of the coop? If they get out a lot, then you don't need a space that is so big.

You should also ensure that that your coop is tall enough for you to walk through as you are inspecting your birds or feeding them.

If you would rather keep your hens locked up all the time in a confined space, you will have to make more adjustments to your coop, which can be a little bit more expensive.

3. Ventilation

Your chicken will generate a lot of moisture from the water vapor from their breath and from their manure. Chicken do not urinate; therefore, their droplets tends to have a lot of moisture that evaporates into the air (75 to 80 percent of moisture).

So the air in the chicken coop gets so humid. Humid air or damp air can be so uncomfortable for your chicken, and also holds a lot of microorganisms such as bacteria and viruses that can be harmful to your chicken and to you.

A well-ventilated coop also takes away ammonia from the chicken poop. Ammonia in the air can cause respiratory problems for your birds.

This is why proper ventilation is so important.

A properly ventilated coop will allow for adequate circulation of fresh air inside the coop and stale damp air out of the coop. In this sequence of events, your coop will be fresh all the time for your chickens.

The ventilation vent should be placed near the ceiling wall above the heads of your chickens. Most coop builders use this rule: 1sq.ft of ventilation per 10sq.ft of floor space if you live in cold areas or during winter.

More vent space is required for people living in warmer areas or during summer.

The window in your coop should be placed at a point that allows for sunlight to enter into your coop for your chickens and to add extra ventilation.

4. Protection

Your coop should provide enough protection for our chicken. Many predators prey for your chicken; they include eagles, hawks, owl, dogs, foxes, cats, snakes, or any other animal that might harm your birds. So if your area is prone to these, make sure to enclose your coop to keep off predators.

So how do you protect your flock?

- Fence the entire chicken run or their coop. This will help keep the hawks or the owls away.

- Raise your coop several feet from the ground and provide your chicken with a ramp to get into their coop. This will help protect against ground animals such as snakes, dogs, raccoons, etc.

- Keep the area around your coop clear. This is because most predators require a place to hide while hunting for the chicken. So if you deny them that pleasure, you have better chances of keeping them away.

- Collect your chickens' eggs at least twice a day. Eggs attract predators, and some of your chicken will lay their eggs just around the run. So you have to pick these eggs up daily to avoid attracting the predators.

5. Temperature

Keeping your chicken in the coop at the right temperature is very essential. The right temperature can increase their egg production, improve their health, and prevent sicknesses or death from extreme cold or hot conditions.

Chicken are comfortable at temperatures of between 12° Celsius (or 55° Fahrenheit) to around 29° Celsius (or 85° Fahrenheit).

Extreme hot or cold conditions could have dire consequences for your birds.

In hot areas or during summer, make sure the ceiling of your chickens' coop is much higher, and adequate ventilation is provided for temperature regulation. Extreme high temperatures can bring more susceptibility to bacterial infections or even death.

Cold weather or season can reduce egg production or even cause frostbites in their feet.

6. Roosting Perch

Roosting perches provide the sleeping areas for the hens when they are old enough to perch. A perch also helps your flock to be up close together and warm each other during the cold seasons. But during warmer conditions, your birds will spread out on the roosting perches.

A suitable perch should allow for 8-12 inches of space per bird. The perch should also be 2-4 inches wide for comfort since chicken sleep flat-footed (this also allows the chicken to spread their weight all through their feet and heel).

Roosting perch should be 18-24 inches from the ground. Higher perches can be dangerous since heavier chickens can injure their feet while attempting to perch when they want to sleep.

Since birds poop at night mostly, you should ensure that you place your roosting perch at a place where you can easily collect the poop in the morning when you are cleaning your perch. Also, keep the roosting perches far from their nest boxes.

Your chicken needs to roost while they sleep rather than just lying on the ground. On the ground, ectoparasites such as lice and mites can easily attack your chicken feet. Also, mice can nibble at their feet at night.

Below is an example of a roost

7. Lighting

Light is essential for your chickens to eat, drink, and even lay eggs.

Lighting can either be natural or artificial. It is essential to reach a standard level of 14 hours of lighting per day.

So why is lighting so important?

- It allows for maximum production of eggs.

- Adequate lighting stimulates sexual maturity

- Lighting also provides some heat during cold seasons.

So go out to your nearby shop and get a 60 Watt bulb if your coop is large (more than 200 square feet) and 40 Watt bulb for a smaller coop.

8. Nesting Boxes

Nesting boxes are where chicken lay their eggs. They are important because your chicken will find it safe and comfortable to lay eggs, and also, you won't have to be searching for eggs around your compound or yard.

You should ensure that you have standard sized nesting boxes of 12 X 12 inches wide.

Your nesting box should be approximately 12 inches above the ground.

You can use one nesting box for three to four chicken, or if you have adequate space, it is much better if you give each chicken its nesting box.

It should be located in the quiet, safe, and darker areas in your coop since chickens love a little privacy when laying their eggs.

Below is an example of a nesting box

9. Bedding Material

Proper bedding material should be able to absorb some moisture, insulate the floor, give them a chance to take a dust bath, make it easier to collect chicken droppings.

The most common chicken bedding material include

• Straw and hay

• Pine shavings

47

- Cedar shavings

- Sand

- Grass clippings

- Shredded leaves

Below is a chicken straw bedding

10. Feeders And Drinkers

Hang your feeders near the ground of your coop at a level that is accessible for all the birds in your coop.

Have some of your feeders on the floor for young chicks.

Always ensure that your feeders are clean and far from where your birds poop the most.

For your drinkers, ensure that they are situated outside and are always clean and replaced with fresh water.

They are kept outside the coop to avoid the accumulation of excess moisture in the air inside the coop due to evaporation.

Feeder

A waterer

11. The Compound Around Your Coop

You should set up your coop in an area with shade.

This can be done by building your coop under a large tree if you happen to have one close to your house, or you can use artificial shades like beside your house, etc.

You should have a dust bathing area for your chicken around your compound close to the coop.

If your chickens are confined, then ensure that you provide them with the dust bath tab in there confinement areas. Chicken take dust baths to control the oils they produce on their bodies. Dust baths also protect them from external parasites and are also a sort of entertainment for your birds.

With all of those important factors with you, let us now discuss a step by step procedure of how you are going to build a coop in the next section.

12. Step By Step Procedure Of Building A Coop

Let us begin with the tools that you will require to build a chicken coop in the section below.

Tools Required:

- Wood such as cedar or redwood

- Screwdriver

- Screw nails

- Woodcutting saw

- Measuring tape and a pencil

- Extension cords

- Hammer

- Spirit level

- Sandpaper

- Paint and a paintbrush

So how do you do it?

Procedure

- Start by setting up four vertical posts on the ground in a rectangular manner or shape.

You could set the distance between the posts to be 8 feet by 16 feet. Or you can choose any measurements based on the size of the coop you need keeping in mind the space requirements per chicken.

- Use the electric stand saw to cut the posts in a manner that the front two posts are 8 feet tall, while the posts at the back are 6 feet tall.

This will later be important because it will allow you to install a pitched roof over the coop's enclosed part.

- Add a post, 2 feet from one of either of the two front posts of the rectangle (let say the right corner). It should be also 8 feet in height.

This will later be used as a gate for the entryway to the run.

- Use the screwdriver to screw in a horizontal position between the right corner front post and the post that we added 2 feet from it.

These screwed points of the two posts should be 6 feet from the ground.

- Build a gate frame at the 6 feet height of our right corner post and the post 2 feet from it. Use lumber to build this frame. Attach the gate frame to the corner post with galvanized gate hinges.

- Add a pair of parallel posts approximately 2.5 feet of the distance from the left front corner of our coop. We need these posts to support the frame of the enclosed portion of the coop.

- Now the front side of our coop has 3 eight-feet tall post and a gate frame.

- Attach a horizontal frame between the tops of all the posts along the front and back sides of your structure. Add three more posts at an angle between the 3 pairs of taller front posts and the shorter rear posts as your rafters.

- Attach a horizontal frame to the four posts on the left side of the rectangle 24 inches from the ground.

  This frame will support the floor of the enclosed area.

- Add a floor plank on top of the lower front frame, two-thirds from the left corner of your coop.

Attach this floor plank with decking screws using your screwdriver.

- Since we will be placing our rooster perch at the back of the coop, cover the back of the floor with a chicken wire mesh. This wire mesh will allow us to collect the chicken droppings from the ground below the coop since they will fall through the chicken wire mesh.

- Dig a 10-inch trench around the perimeter of the chicken run.

- Install a chicken wire in the trench you have dug and cover it with soil to prevent animals that might dig through it and attack your chicken.

  Your structure will look like the picture below when you are done

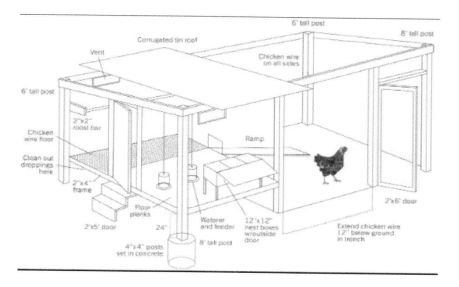

Now that you have built your chicken a perfect home, you need to figure out what you will feed them after you buy them. In the next chapter, I will show you the best meals for your chicken.

13. Nutrition And Feeding Of Chicken

Just like human beings, chickens also require a balanced diet to grow healthily and fast. A well-fed bird will thrive, produce adequate healthy eggs, and delicious meat.

Chicken are omnivores, so their feed should have adequate proportions of proteins, carbohydrates, vitamins, and minerals.

Chicken eat a lot of different kinds of substances such as vegetable leaves, insects, grubs, cooked beans, seeds, and fruits.

Some foods should be avoided, such as citrus fruits, avocado, garlic, uncooked beans, green potato skins, and onions as they are unhealthy to your chicken, sometimes even poisonous.

Protein is very important for the growth of your chickens and for producing eggs. If you have a layer, give it adequate amounts of proteins, and you will be so happy with the outcome.

It is important to let your chicken walk around and forage for their food but don't let them depend on that solely because it is not enough. Give them some more feeds from the shop.

Feeds are given based upon their age i.e.

- **Chicks** - From when they are hatched to when they are 6 weeks old, they will need to be fed chick crumbs. Chick crumbs are highly nutritious chick feeds that are formulated to provide a complete balanced diet for chicks. The nutrients in them promote good health, muscle, and skeletal development. They also have carbohydrates for energy to promote growth and also have vitamins and minerals.

So if you have chicks in your coop, get yourself chick crumbs and watch how healthily your birds will grow and develop.

- **Pullet** – there are 6-18 weeks old hens. During this period, chicken do lots of growing; therefore, you need to feed them with a meal that helps them to do that.

For this type of chicken, you need to feed them with Grower's pellets or Grower's mash.

They have a high protein quantity of approximately 16 percent. Grower's pellets or Grower's mash will provide adequate amounts of essential amino acids that help support the rapid growth of tissue, muscle and skeleton as the bird grows.

Grower's pellets also have a highly digestible cooked wheat, which helps to provide the energy required for growth. It also contains an organic acidifier that helps reduce the risk of bacterial or fungal infections from the feed itself, and in doing so, it also helps to benefit gut health.

- **Laying hens/Adult hens** – these are chicken that are over 18 weeks old.

  This group of chicken is fed "Layers' Pellets." Layers' pellets are formulated to provide a complete balanced diet for all types of adult and laying chickens.

  It has approximately 15-17 percent protein, which is essential for egg production, tissue, and feather production.

  It has micronized wheat for carbohydrate energy and for fiber.

  It also has Omega 6 fatty acids, which help maximize egg production and is rich in natural plant extras such as paprika and marigold, which have been proven to help produce rich golden yolk color in eggs.

  In addition to vitamins and minerals, it also has organic selenium, which supports the body's antioxidant defense system and immunity as well as eggshell integrity.

14. Grit

One critical factor when feeding your chicken is to ensure that they have adequate **grit**. Grit refers to the small stones that chicken usually eat.

As you well know, chickens do not have teeth; they swallow whatever they eat. They need the grit to grind up food in their gizzard. This helps the chicken in digesting the food that they eat.

So you must ensure that you give your chickens adequate amount of grit, since this is so essential to them.

You can purchase grit with oyster shells (is highly recommended) since the oyster shells provide calcium that is essential to enable your chickens to lay eggs with strong shells.

15. Water

Water is also essential for your chicken; no living organism can survive without water.

Chicken need about 500ml to 1 liter of clean drinking water per day.

Keep changing the water to keep it fresh for the chickens and also wash the waterer as often as you can.

16. So How Much Of These Feeds Will Your Chicken Require In A Day?

Chicks require a constant supply of chick crumbs per day.

Pullets also require a constant supply of their meals per day since they are rapidly growing during this age; therefore, you have to give them meals to keep up with their fast-growing rate.

Laying hens will require approximately 120 grams of layers pellets per day.

You can also occasionally throw in vegetable leaves, like kales, cabbages, etc. to enrich their diet.

Provide them with maize grains too, which they seem to love; it has adequate carbohydrates and proteins for your chicken. Just a handful per day is enough since maize/corn grains have a high amount of fats.

Invest in quality feeders and waterer to ensure minimum wastage of the feeds and water. A quality feeder keeps the chicken feed dry always.

17. How To Feed Your Chicken While They Are Molting

During cold seasons like winter, chicken shed their feathers and regrow them. This process is known as molting, and it takes 2 to 3 months.

Usually, it occurs after the chickens have finished laying eggs, and they do not lay any egg during this period. Molting is crucial because it helps the chicken to discard broken old/tired feathers and helps chicken to replace these old features with fresh new tight feathering, which insulates them properly against elements such as wind, rain, and snow.

They are very dull, semi bald, and shivering during this period.

So how do you feed them during this period?

- Feed them a high protein diet such as cottonseed meal, sunflower meal, peanut meals, sesame meal, and Alfalfa meal. High protein diet is very important since chicken use a lot of protein to rebuild their new feathers. Feathers are 85 percent protein.

- Make their feed easily available to them 24 hours a day.

- When the molting period is over, gradually bring their diet to be normal and get them more energy-based feeds to get them back on their feet as easy and quickly as possible.

Also, it is important to reduce or stop handling chicken while they molt; this is because the area that the feather shaft meets the skin is very sensitive during this period. Touching this area can be very painful.

Now that your birds have a house and food, how are you going to take care of them?

You will learn all about taking care of your chicken in the next chapter.

Caring For Your Chicken

There are tasks that you need to do to keep your chicken healthy, comfortable, and safe. Caring for your chicken will be very rewarding to you and to your chicken. The good thing is that caring for chicken does not a lot of time.

1. Dialy Care For Your Chicken:

- The first thing you need to do as a chicken farmer is to ensure that your chickens have plenty of food and freshwater. Feeding them regularly will keep them healthy, growing, happy, and more productive.

  Providing clean, freshwater in a clean container is also crucial. Water is essential in hydration and for facilitating/supporting all the essential body processes. Therefore, ensure that water is always available and served clean and fresh.

- Ensure that there is grit around your coop or in your coop. Grit is essential for your birds since it is essential in grinding up of all the food in the chickens' gizzard.

- Spot check your chickens' coop once or twice daily, to ensure that it is always clean and sanitary. Change the bedding, or sweep your coop if it happens to be dirty with poop. Keep on changing the waterer and the feeder as often as you can. This will help you to keep your chickens clean and healthy because a clean coop reduces the chances of diseases.

- Empty the nesting box of any eggs your chicken has left for you. Collecting eggs frequently ensures that you get clean eggs. It also minimizes the cracking of the egg or chances of eggs going stale. Emptying the nesting boxes also encourages your chicken to bring forth more eggs. When your chickens are ready for brooding, leave just enough for them for this purpose - your hens also expect to have their own chicks after the end of their laying period.

- If you are letting your birds free-range, you know, run a little and search for other meals they might be interested in, be sure to leave the door of the coop open at all times. This will enable them to enter and leave the coop as they please, more so when one wants to lay an egg.

If you like your birds enclosed, then just monitor them closely in their coop.

- Count your chickens at the end of each day to keep a record of your birds and to ensure that none of them is lost. Doing this will also help you to know if all your birds are okay and healthy.

- Ensure that the door and the windows to your coop are closed to prevent predators from coming in.

2. Monthly Chicken Care Tasks

- Change the bedding of your chicken every month. The state of your bedding largely depends on the daily cleaning of your chicken droppings. Allow your chicken to have a comfortable dry bedding always.

- You should also sanitize the feeders and waterers monthly. This will promote the health of your chicken tremendously.

You can use bleach as your sanitizer by mixing 1 part of bleach to 9 parts of water, i.e., 100ml of bleach added to 900ml of water. This will give you a ten percent bleach sanitizer. This percentage is safe and very effective in clearing out microorganisms that pose threat to your birds.

- Freshen your nesting boxes once a month. You can do this by removing poop and broken eggshells from the nesting boxes. This will give your chicken a cleaner environment to lay eggs and brood in. A new nesting box reduces the chances of infections to your unhatched chicks and the mother hen.

- Stock up on supplies needed by your chickens. For example, get enough chicken feed for your flock.

3. Semiyearly Chicken Care Tasks

- Once or twice a year, always make sure that you deep clean and sanitize your chicken coop.

  Wash down the walls, all the surfaces, and every corner of your coop using ten percent bleach.

  Whenever there is an infection, you can do this as well, to reduce the spread and to prevent the re-occurrence of the infection.

- Do proper maintenance in your coop. Look out for week hinges, pointy nails, broken wood logs, or weak wood surfaces. Make sure the chicken wire is all fine and strong.

Ensure that the roofing is intact, ventilation is fine, your lighting system works fine, and your window and doors are all operating perfectly too.

- If you live in areas that experience winter, you have to prepare for winter. You can do this by ensuring that you have enough roosting space for all your chicken, because chickens roost together to stay warm.

Ensure that you have heaters for your waterers.

Have a bulb switched on 16 hours lighting per day to promote egg-laying, growth, and development of your chicken.

4. How To Catch, Handle Or Hold Your Chicken

I saw an interesting question during my research on this book. A couple of people asked, on various articles, "How do I hold my Chicken?"

So I was encouraged to put in a little section on how to do it. It is a pretty simple technique that you will master after a few steps.

How do you do it?

- Throw your chicken a few food pellets like maize grains, and they will come running towards you.

- Usher your chicken into a corner before trying to pick them up.

- Use your powerful hand, the one you write with, and place it on the back of your chicken, securing their wings as much as possible. Do not grab their wings or the tail feathers, because this will be very uncomfortable for them.

- With your other hand, secure their legs and their lower body and gently and carefully lift them up.

- Hold them under your arm firmly to make it difficult for them to flap about or jump down, which can cause injury to them. Also, pet them to give them a sense of security by calming their nerves and familiarize them with a human touch.

There are a few things you should refrain from when handling your chicken:

- Avoid chasing your chicken when you want to catch them. This will make them skittish and stressed, leading to further health conditions.

- Never pick up a chicken by its feet or its neck, as this can cause them both physical and mental stress.

Next, we will discuss how you stand to benefit by rearing chicken.

Pros And Cons Of Raising A Chicken

1. The Pros

There are very many benefits of raising chickens. Here are just but a few mentions:

- The number one benefit that comes with raising chicken is that **chickens lay eggs**. Their eggs will be fresh, delicious, and nutritious.

  The quality of eggs depends on the quality of food that you give your chickens and also what they eat by themselves while foraging, like insects, greens, etc. Expect one egg per day from each chicken that you have. Raise good breeds known for laying eggs, e.g., the Golden Comet Breed, Rhode Island breed, etc. and you will thank yourself for raising chicken.

- **Chickens are the best-known source of white meat.** White meat is the healthiest and recommended type of meat. And home grown chicken have a better-richer taste compared to those that are factory farmed.

- From the first two points, we can see that chickens are a great **source of money**. You can earn money by selling some of your eggs or some of your hens if they become overpopulated. Some people also buy chicken droppings as manure to make their soil more fertile.

- **Chickens poop/droppings are a great fertilizer.** Chicken manure is a natural, quality raw fertilizer that potassium, phosphorus and high amounts of nitrogen. These minerals are the main ingredients in garden and lawn fertilizers that are processed and sold at shops. You can compost chicken manure, and then you can add it to your garden, trees, lawns, shrubs, flowerpots etc.

This natural fertilizer will save you money and help produce great results. Natural manure from your chicken will improve the soil in your garden and ensure the continuous production of nutrients to your crops since they provide nutrients slowly.

- **Chickens also make great pets**. After getting used to your chicken, you will see that they make a wonderful pet. They have their personalities and are affectionate towards human beings. I find it so therapeutic just watching my birds run around, play, mingle, and eat together. In due time, you will find yourself enjoying the company of your chicken and having a lot of fun with them.

- Chickens also assist you in **cleaning your yard or your compound**. They will do this by clearing the harvested garden beds of weeds, grains and eat fallen fruit from trees before they rot and attract bugs.

  Chickens can literally eat any organic stuff that you normally would throw away like food scraps such as seeds, nuts, vegetable peelings, rice, fruits, salads, leftovers and much more. Eating these items enriches their diet, and by doing this, your chicken will become **your natural waste disposal team**.

- **Chickens are the easiest and relatively cheap animals to take care of** as compared to other animals. They are low-maintenance animals with great returns. They simply need to be watered, fed, and housed in a coop where they nest. And sometimes, you give them just a little meal per day, and they graze outside and get more to their fill.

- Bugs such as crickets, grasshoppers, snails, slugs and other pests in your garden are eaten up by chickens as a source of protein. They also eat weeds around your yard or compound. By doing this, **chickens naturally control bugs and weeds** around your house or your garden. This can help you save up on insecticides and herbicides.

- Chicken, mostly male hens, roosters, can serve as your alarm clock in the morning. Rosters are known to crow at the same time every morning, usually at first light.

There are a few cons that I will explain below that come with the raising of chicken. This will get you prepared and ready to deal with your chickens.

2. The Cons

They include:

- **Chickens are noisy**. This everyone can agree with. They make rather annoying sounds that may sound like "buck, buck, buck, bugawk."

These noises require some getting used to.

But fortunately, they also provide quieter sounds like clucking, cooing and various other sounds that some people find relaxing.

- Chicken fertilizer is made using chicken poop. **Chicken droppings are very smelly and gross** and can sometimes contain harmful microorganisms. But remember that chicken poop makes a great fertilizer that will go a long way in getting you the ideal garden/lawn you want. To get this fertilizer, you need to put in a lot of work, bear with the smell and ugliness of the chicken poop, get protective clothing (which includes protective farm gloves, gumboots, and an apron).

- **Chicken feed attracts rodents**. So you will have to also deal with rodents or prevent them from coming into your home.

- Chickens will dig a lot while they are living with you, therefore, **making your backyard ugly**. Chickens scratch when they dig for bugs, sometimes when they want to take a dust bath and can really mess up your yard or your compound pace. If you have a lawn and an open backyard garden, chicken can turn it upside down by eating everything and digging up what's left. You have to fence the garden.

- **Chickens can carry Salmonella bacteria**. These bacteria can cause infections to you too. Chickens carry

Salmonella germs in their droppings, their feathers, feet, and beaks. That is why it is important to practice good hygiene (where you wash your hands frequently whenever you handle chicken or surfaces where they have been). This will help you to minimize the risk of infection.

- Just like other pets or farm animals, **chickens require proper health care, which can be expensive.** They need to be treated, vaccinated, and protected against infections. When chickens get sick or injured, you may be required to visit professional pet care. The most common chicken illnesses include diseases like respiratory problems, mites, a prolapsed vent, bumble foot and more.

- **Chickens grow old and die in just about 8 to 10 years.** As they grow older, egg production decreases. Peak egg production will start when the chicken is one year old and last for 2 to 3 years. It is important that you still continue to care for them responsibly as they old, or you can decide to use them for meat production.

- **Chickens can be mean to each other sometimes.** You will notice some chickens bullying each other. They will fight with each other or peck at each other and even draw blood. The fighting can be serious sometimes to point where one dies. To avoid this, keep the bully chicken separate from other humble chickens. Or you can sell it if you have a buyer.

- Chickens and **their habitat or environment need regular cleanup.** Chickens can be dirty sometimes, pooping everywhere and in turn, creating messes, so you will need to regularly clean chickens, their coops, and their bedding material. It is hard to train a chicken the way we train our dogs, so you just have to bear with their mess. Get good bedding for your chicken, one that can be easily replaced and even cleaned.

- **Chicken predators.** If your yard is accessible to predators such as your dog, cat, or your neighbors' dogs or cats, foxes, raccoons, hawks, eagles, snakes, skunks, possums, coyotes, or other animals, this can pose a threat to the safety of your chickens. You will have to get a good fence, train your dog to be friendly with the chicken, put quality chicken wire around your chicken run, and at the end of each day, make sure that every one of your birds is back in the coop.

- **Basic requirements for your chickens' comfortable well-being such as chicken feed, vaccines, etc. might be pretty expensive**. Give your chicken a constant supply of water, grit and feed, (grit refers to the small rocks to help them digest their food).

- **Chickens require a shelter that can be expensive to obtain or to build**. You will have to create your own coop or buy a coop if you don't have all the requirements needed to build a coop. After getting a coop, you need to maintain it for it to support your chicken for a long time.

- Chickens require other chickens for companionship because they are social animals. **So you cannot keep only one chicken because it can die of loneliness**. So when you want to start raising chickens, make sure that you have a good number of them so that they can provide companionship for each other. A flock of chicken will be happy, healthy, and more productive.

- **Laws in your state**: Check with the county or state regulations to know what the law says about rearing chicken. This is especially important if you live in towns/cities, as some by-laws may have special requirements regarding rearing chicken.

Next, we will discuss how to deal with various diseases and treat your chicken whenever they are ill.

Common Chicken Diseases, Treatments, And Vaccine

When raising chickens, you need to be able to recognize your chickens' disease from an early onset of symptoms and know how best you can treat them when they contract a disease.

The following are the more common types of diseases that attack chickens and how you can handle them.

1. Fowl Pox

If you have noticed that your chickens' skin has some white spots, white ulcers on their trachea and mouth or scabby sores on their combs, this could be a sign of Fowl Fox disease. It is also often accompanied by reduction in egg laying.

79

This disease, or rather the virus causing it, can be spread from one chicken to another when the infected chicken comes into contact with healthy ones. It can also be contracted by a vector such as mosquitos, as well as through air.

You can treat Fowl Pox disease by feeding your chickens' soft food and providing them with a warm and dry place to recover by themselves. With adequate care, your birds can survive this illness.

If you would like to remove the odds of your birds even contracting this disease, there is a vaccine available. The vaccine is simply known as "Fowl Pox Vaccine." It is recommended for healthy chickens aged eight weeks or older and four weeks before the start of laying of eggs.

Ask for directions and dosage on how to apply this vaccine from where you purchase it.

<u>Caution When Giving The Vaccine:</u>

Avoid hitting large blood vessels, bones, and the wing muscles with the double-needle applicator during vaccination. Do not inject in any other site except the exposed wing web

Examine the site of vaccine administration 6 - 8 days after vaccination. A positive vaccine take (showing successful vaccination), is indicated by swelling or formation of a nodular lesion at the site of inoculation.

Swelling and scabs will disappear at about two weeks following vaccination.

The absence of lesion may indicate that the birds were immune before vaccination or that improper vaccination methods were used.

2. Bumblefoot

Bumblefoot is a chicken disease caused by Staphylococcus bacteria, which enters the chicken through a cut, scratch, or injury in their foot.

This disease begins when your chickens accidentally injure (cut) their feet. It can happen any time while they are busy foraging and scratching the ground.

The cut then gets infected. And your chicken's foot begins to swell due to the development of an abscess full of pus.

You will notice your chicken limping more often or even rest most of the time to avoid the pain in their feet. You will also notice a swelling of the joints in the toes and foot of your chicken.

After noticing these signs, inspect the foot of your chicken and take action as quickly as possible before it extends up the leg of your chicken.

What makes your chicken more susceptible to bumblefoot?

- When their roosts are too high - jumping can cause an injury to their feet, something that may open a door to the bacteria.

- If your chicken bedding is hard-packed, or made up of rough material, your chicken can get injured when they jump on it.

- They can also injure their feet from a rough roost.

- Walking around on a wet, soiled bedding for a long time can make it easier for bacteria to penetrate through.

Preventive Measures Against Bumblefoot

- Roosts should be rounded or flat, free of rough spots and located approximately 2 feet from the ground

- Keep the chicken coop bedding clean and dry as possible. Also, use soft bedding like wood shavings.

- Inspect the free-ranging areas of your chicken to see if there exists any sharp objects can injure their feet.

- Perform regular checkups on your chicken feet for earlier identification of the disease.

Treatment Of Bumblefoot

- The beginning stages of bumblefoot can be easily treated. Just fill a basin with warm water and Epsom salts and soak the infected foot for ten minutes. Dry the foot gently and apply an antibacterial agent such as Vetericyn, NuStock or honey. Cover with a little wrap and give it a day or two to heal.

- In later stages of bumblefoot, only treatment for this disease is through surgery i.e. cutting off the infected part. If you don't do this, this infection will take over the chicken and claim its life.

Bumblefoot can happen very easily, and there isn't much you can do to prevent it besides just keeping a close eye on your chickens' feet. If you notice they have a cut, then make sure you wash and disinfect it to prevent this disease from setting up.

3. Fowl Cholera/Avian Cholera

Signs
Equate Fowl Cholera

Swellings of comb and wattles   Mouth and nasal discharge

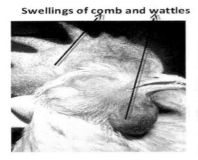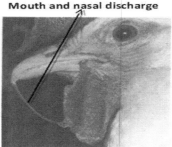

Fowl cholera is a serious and highly contagious disease caused by a bacteria known as *Pasteurella multocida*. Older chickens are more susceptible to this disease than younger ones.

This disease can range from acute septicemia (acute poisoning of the blood due to bacterial toxins) to chronic and localized infections.

The route of infection of this deadly bacteria is through the oral or nasal route. After it has infected your chicken, it will incubate for 5-8 days before it starts exhibiting symptoms.

You should be suspicious of this disease:

- If you notice a swelling on their wattles or faces

- If they have a yellowish or greenish

- If they cough often

- If they don't eat well – a sign that they have reduced appetite

- If they seem to be having joint pain

- If the birds seem to be having breathing problems

- If their head or wattle is darkened

The bacteria is often contracted from contaminated food and water or from wild animals.

Treatment And Vaccination

When your chicken gets this disease, treat them with sulphonamides, tetracycline, or any other antibiotics. But unfortunately, if your chicken recovers, it will remain a carrier of this disease.

A vaccine can be administered orally at six weeks of your chicken's age. The name of the vaccine is "Attenuated Live Fowl Cholera M-3-G."

Prevention And Control Of This Disease

Prevention of this disease is through:

- Observing good sanitation

- Rodent control since they are the vectors of this disease

- Separation of birds through age since the older ones are the highly susceptible ones.

Control of this disease is by the culling of the affected flock. This is where you separate the infected flock and kill them in the nicest way and disposing of their bodies in a place that can't be reached. This is because the bacteria tends to still live on in their dead bodies even after death.

4. Infectious Coryza

Infectious Coryza is caused by a bacterium known as *Haemophilus paragallinarum*.

The route of transmission of this disease is through interaction with infected chicken or carriers. In can be through Airborne droplets, drinking contaminated water, and also through direct interaction.

Here are some of the common signs and symptoms of the disease:

- If your chicken's heads become swollen

- If their wattles also swell

- If they are sneezing

- A sharp reduction in their egg production

- Dysponea (this is difficulty in breathing), and

- If their eyes are shut and swollen – often accompanied by discharge coming from the nose and eyes

- Having moisture under the wings

The vaccine for Infectious Coryza is "Coryza Gel -3^R".

Treatment is done using antibiotics such as Erythromycin, sulfonamides, tylosin, etc.

Control And Prevention Of Infectious Coryza

Once your chickens contract this disease, they should be put down. If not, they will remain a carrier of the disease for life, which is a risk to the rest of your chicken.

Be sure to discard the body afterward to avoid other chicken from getting infected by it.

As such, ensure your chicken don't come into contact with other random chicken and keep their coop clean. Moreover, ensure that you give them clean water. All these measures will help you protect them from contracting the disease in the first place.

5. Botulism

This disease is caused by bacteria known as *Clostridium botulinum.*

If your chickens begin to have progressing tremors, a soiled beak, or when your broilers tend to settle with eyes closed, you should grow concerned. If your chickens have botulism, the tremors will progress into total body paralysis, which also includes cessation of their breathing. You will also notice that their feathers will be easy to pull out, and death usually occurs within a few hours.

It is a serious disease.

But what can you do about it?

Well, there is an antitoxin that can be purchased from your local vet although it is considered to be expensive. However, if you catch the disease early enough, you can mix 1 teaspoon of Epsom salts with 1 ounce of warm water, then give it to them by dropper once daily.

How to control Botulism:

- Remove any dead bird in your compound or where your chicken forage.

- Supply clean water and feed. You can do this by feeding your birds in containers rather than the ground.

- Drain any stagnant water in your compound.

- In simple terms, just have a clean compound all the time.

6. Mushy Chick/Omphalitis

The disease results from a bacterial infection of the yolk sac, which explains why it is predominantly common among chicks. More precisely, it is common among chicks that have been hatched artificially. Some of the common bacteria responsible for the disease include *E. coli, Staphylococci, Proteus and Pseudomonas.*

Common Signs And Symptoms:

- Chicks with this disease tend to have a navel that is inflamed and does not close, often with a tint of blue.

- Chicks tend to appear weak, drowsy and with an unpleasant smell.

- The chicks don't gain weight as fast as healthy chicks.

Prevention

- Ensure that the sanitation, humidity and temperature within the incubator is optimal.

- Don't put dirty, cracked eggs in your incubator

- Clean the incubator and sanitizer it thoroughly before you put in new eggs.

- And make sure to isolate chicks that look sickly

Treatment

Although sometimes antibiotics are used and may seem to work, there is no actual treatment for this disease.

This disease does affect humans so be careful when handling poultry suffering from the disease.

7. Marek's Disease

This disease is like a chickens' version of man's herpes disease.

This disease is more common in younger birds that are usually under the age of 20 weeks.

Common symptoms include the following:

- A sudden onset of tumors outside or inside your flock

- A sudden change of iris to gray

- Tendency to not respond to light

- Paralysis of wings and legs

Unfortunately, this disease is very easy to catch. It is a virus, which means it is super easy to transmit from bird to bird.

They obtain the virus by breathing in pieces of shed skin and feathers from an infected chick.

The route of infection of this disease is usually respiratory.

It spreads easily by infective feather-docile dander or fomites. Infected birds remain viraemic for life.

There is no treatment for this disease; however, there is a vaccine (1500 PFU of HVT), and it is usually given to day-old chicks.

The disease can also be prevented by maintaining hygiene.

8. Newcastle Disease

This disease is caused by the Newcastle Disease Virus.

Some of the signs and symptoms include the following:

- Breathing problems

- Murky looking eyes

- Rapid decline in eggs production (some even stop laying)

- Discharge from their nose

- Paralysis of the wings and legs

- Twisting of neck

Wild birds tend to be carriers of the disease so be sure to avoid or minimize contact between your flock and wild birds. Even so, it important to note that you could also transmit the disease to other birds by simply touching or interacting with infected birds as it may stick on your shoes, clothes and other items hence the need to observe high levels of hygiene.

However, the good news is that older birds usually recover, and they won't carriers afterward.

But most baby birds will die from the disease.

There is a vaccine for the disease; it is called "Newcastle Disease Vaccine LaSota Strain." Vaccinate your healthy chicken when they are 14 days of age and revaccinate when they are 4 weeks and 16 weeks of age.

9. Thrush/Candidiasis

This disease is caused by a fungal yeast, *Candida albicans.*

The route of infection is oral, i.e., through the beaks when drinking unsanitary water.

Common signs and symptoms include:

- Oozing of something on the space between the neck and body (the crop).

- Increased appetite

- Increased lethargy

- Crusty vent

- Feathers that look ruffled

Thrush is a fungal disease, which means you could easily make your chickens to develop it if you allow them to eat anything that has mold, contaminated surfaces and water.

As such, as a fungal disease, you can use anti-fungal medication like Nystatin, which you can get from your local vet. There is no vaccine for this.

To prevent infection, be sure to remove the bad food and clean their water container as well.

10. Air Sac Disease

This disease is caused by bacteria known as *Mycoplasma gallisepticum.*

Some of the common signs include:

- Poor form when laying eggs

- Chicken appearing too weak

- Breathing problems

- Swollen joints

- Sneezing

- Coughing

- Death

It can be treated with a broad-spectrum antibiotic such as Tylosin, Terramycin and Gallimycin, either in their feed, drinking water or by injection.

Your chickens could get this disease from other birds (like wild birds) or your chicks could be hatched with it (a hen can lay infected eggs).

So just keep an eye out for any of these symptoms so it can be treated quickly and effectively.

11. Avian Influenza

Avian Influenza is most commonly known as bird flu.

You can also contract this disease from your chicken.

However, after knowing the symptoms, you'll be able to put that fear to rest.

Common signs and symptoms include the following:

- Respiratory problems

- Sharp decline in the number of eggs that a hen lays (some even stop laying)

- Diarrhea

- Swelling on the part of the chicken's face

- Discolored wattle and comb (it may turn blue)

- Dark red spots that appear mostly on the comb and legs

Vaccines for this virus are available and used mainly during a breakout. Inactivated forms of the virus are used as the vaccine.

Practice exclusion biosecurity as a preventive measure during a breakout.

And also, once your birds get this disease, they need to be put down and the carcass destroyed. And you will need to sanitize any area that the birds were in before ever introducing a new flock.

12. Pullorum

The disease manifests differently depending on the age of the chicken.

For chicks:

- There may be no sign of activity

- There may be a white paste on their backsides

- There may be signs of breathing difficulties

- Some chicks may die even without symptoms

For older chicken:

- There may be coughing

- Sneezing

- And poor laying skills.

This is a viral disease.

Your birds can contract it from contaminated surfaces or oven other birds (mostly wild birds) that have grown somewhat immune to the disease but are carriers.

There is no vaccine for this one unfortunately.

If your chicken contracts it, all you have left to do is to put it down and destroy its carcass well by burying it at least 2 feet deep or burning its carcass. This will ensure no other animal contracts it.

13. Infectious Bronchitis

This is a highly contagious viral respiratory disease of chicken. Even though it is respiratory, it also infects the urogenital and the gastrointestinal tracts.

A type of coronavirus causes this disease.

Some of the common signs and symptoms include:

- Snoring

- Sneezing

- Coughing

These are not conclusive though – you have to get lab tests done to confirm whether your chicken have this virus.

But the good news is you can get a vaccine to stop this disease from impacting your chickens. Infectious Bronchitis is a viral disease and will travel quickly through the air.

To treat Infectious Bronchitis, give your chickens a warm, dry place to recover while providing antibiotics in their drinks.

Recovered birds are immune but are carriers of the disease. The disease will only reoccur when your chickens are under respiratory stress.

The preventive measures are good ventilation and optimal temperature conditions.

So which diseases can you get from your chicken?

Let us discuss this in the next section.

1. Zoonotic Diseases From Chicken

A zoonotic disease is a disease that can be passed from animals (in this case, your chicken) to humans.

These diseases are caused by microorganisms such as viruses, bacteria, parasites, and fungi from your chicken.

You can contract this zoonotic disease through:

- Direct contact with chicken that are infected.

- Aid of an insect, for example, a fly, (which in this case we will call it a vector-borne disease).

- Body fluids and waste from infected birds

- Contact with soil or water that has been contaminated by animal waste that is infected

- By eating meat from infected chicken or by eating food such as fruits and vegetables that have been contaminated by infected animal waste.

Examples of those diseases include.

Influenza (Including H5N1 And H1N1)

Influenza A avian viruses is responsible for causing the Avian (bird) flu. These viruses exist naturally among birds.

Wild birds all over the world are known to be the carriers for this virus (it exists mostly in their intestines) though they don't get sick.

The disease is however very contagious among birds and causes widespread deaths of domesticated birds so you should be careful with your chicken.

When birds are infected, they often shed the virus through their feces, nasal secretions and saliva. It is through these methods that your chicken may be infected – through direct contact with an infected bird (wild or domestic) or through coming into contact with surfaces or feces that have the virus.

Farmers get the disease by being in contact with their chicken. Here is how to go about staying safe:

- Avoid contact with birds or surfaces that may have the virus

- Disinfect surfaces and avoid contact with feces from infected birds

2. Psittacosis

Psittacosis is a bacterial disease that affects all the birds that we keep in our homes, for this case, your chicken.

This infection can be acquired when you inhale dried secretions from infected birds.

Common Signs And Symptoms Include:

- Dry cough

- Muscle aches

- Headache

- Fever

- Pneumonia

- Other complications or even death

The danger about this is that infected birds are often asymptomatic.

3. Salmonellosis

Salmonellosis is a bacterial disease.

Some of the common signs and symptoms include:

- Stomach pains

- Fever

- Diarrhea

In many cases, these symptoms disappear in about a week. However, there may be cases where someone may need hospitalization when the diarrhea does not disappear or if the infection has affected various organs badly

You can get salmonellosis by eating food that is contaminated, such as chicken or eggs.

To reduce infection risks, you should:

- Maintain proper hygiene where you wash your hands regularly using soap whenever you interact closely with any animal (chicken, sheep, goats, cows, horses, pigs, reptiles and other pets) whether feeding, caring or touching them. This is especially critical if you've handled their wastes.

- Children under 5 years of age should not handle the chickens or do so only under parental supervision, and everyone should wash their hands thoroughly afterward.

- Keep your birds in their coop, to reduce the risk of illness.

- When cleaning the chicken feeder, be extra careful to use a separate sink or tub. You don't want to use the same sink you put your own utensils in or where you bath.

- Cook your meat, poultry and eggs thoroughly.

- Make sure to wash vegetables and fruits thoroughly before you eat them. Don't stop there; also clean any surfaces where you prepare food – especially after preparing such raw foods like meats (fish, poultry or red meat). And ensure to wash your hands thereafter before you can handle other foods.

Conclusion

Raising chicken is an art that is both therapeutic, rewarding, and that will also make you feel good and happy about yourself. It will give you or your kids a good sense of responsibility and caring for something deeply.

Lucky for you, this book has explained everything you need to do to care for your chicken like a pro, deal with diseases, and all possible problems you may experience along the way!